Snowman Advent

Design by Joan Green

Size: 5¾ inches W x 20½ inches H
(14.6cm x 52.1cm)
Skill Level: Beginner

Materials

- ❏ 1 artist-size sheet clear 7-count plastic canvas
- ❏ Red Heart Classic Art. E267 medium weight yarn as listed in color key
- ❏ Red Heart Super Saver Art. E300 medium weight yarn as listed in color key
- ❏ 5¾ yards (5.3m) ⅛-inch-wide (6mm) red satin ribbon
- ❏ ¾-inch (19mm) gold jingle bell
- ❏ 25 round plastic-wrapped peppermint candies
- ❏ Sawtooth hanger
- ❏ Sharp sewing needle and thread (optional)
- ❏ #16 tapestry needle
- ❏ Hot-glue gun (optional)

Stitching Step by Step

1 Cut snowman advent calendar from plastic canvas, joining graphs for top and bottom portions before cutting as one piece.

2 Stitch snowman according to graphs, filling in uncoded area on head with white Continental Stitches.

3 Overcast edges according to graph.

4 *When background stitching is complete, work embroidery stitches using a full strand of yarn:* Straight Stitch stripes on scarf using cherry red. Backstitch and Straight Stitch mouth and eyebrows using black. Work white French Knots on snowman's body, wrapping yarn twice around needle for each knot.

5 *Work remaining embroidery stitches using 2 plies separated from a length of yarn:* Using white throughout, Straight Stitch snowflakes on ends of scarf. Work French Knots at ends of snowflake "arms" and in center of snowflake, wrapping yarn once around needle for each knot. Work French Knots on mittens and red hatband, wrapping yarn once around needle. Using black, Backstitch details on arms and scarf.

Assembly

1 Cut ribbon into 25 (8-inch/20.3cm) pieces.

2 Thread one piece of ribbon through hanger on jingle bell. Thread ribbon ends under stitches on reverse side at tip of cap; knot ribbon ends, allowing jingle bell to dangle freely.

3 One by one, thread ends of remaining ribbon pieces through stitched snowman from back to front where indicated by pairs of lavender dots on graph.

4 Beginning at the bottom, tie a wrapped candy to snowman with each pair of ribbon ends, tying ends in a bow.

5 Stitch or hot-glue sawtooth hanger to reverse side of snowman near top.

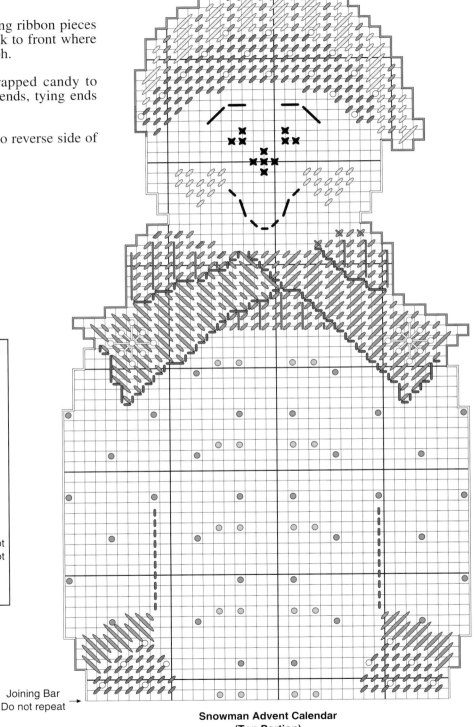

COLOR KEY

Yards	Medium Weight Yarn
56 (51.3m)	□ White #1
2 (1.9m)	■ Black #312
1 (1m)	□ Pink #737
2 (1.9m)	▨ Delft blue #885
10 (9.2m)	□ Blue #886
6 (5.5m)	▨ Cherry red #912

Uncoded area on head is white #1 Continental Stitches
◜ White #1 (2-ply) Straight Stitch
◜ Black #312 (4-ply) Backstitch and Straight Stitch
◜ Black #312 (2-ply) Backstitch
◜ Cherry red #912 Straight Stitch
○ White #1 (2-ply, 1-wrap) French Knot
● White #1 (4-ply, 2-wrap) French Knot
● Attach peppermint candy

Color numbers given are for Red Heart Classic Art. E267 and Super Saver Art. E300 medium weight yarn.

Joining Bar
Do not repeat →

**Snowman Advent Calendar
(Top Portion)**
38 holes x 137 holes
Cut 1
Join with bottom portion
before cutting as 1 piece

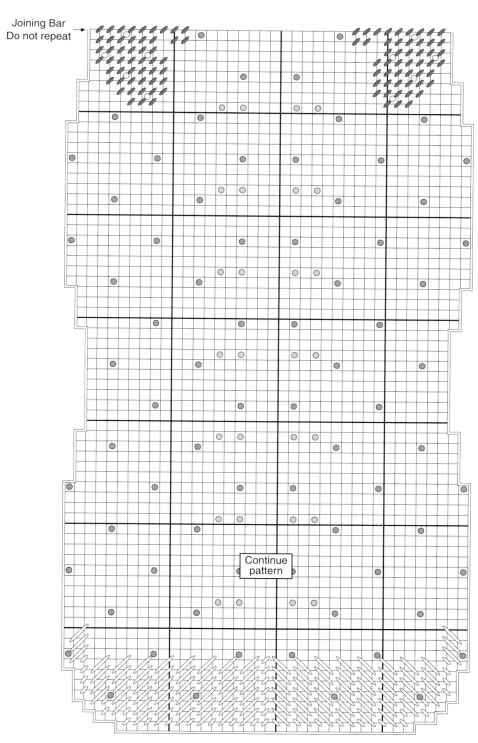

Continue
pattern

Snowman Advent Calendar
(Bottom Portion)
38 holes x 137 holes
Cut 1

Snowman Wind Chime

Design by Kathy Wirth

Size: 7⅞ inches W x 7½ inches H (20cm x 19.1cm), excluding chimes and earmuffs

Skill Level: Beginner

Materials

- ❑ ½ sheet clear 7-count plastic canvas
- ❑ 2 (6-inch) Uniek QuickShape plastic canvas radial circles
- ❑ Uniek Needloft plastic canvas yarn as listed in color key
- ❑ Uniek Needloft metallic craft cord as listed in color key
- ❑ 2 (½-inch) iridescent purple pompoms
- ❑ Silver tinsel stem
- ❑ 4 aluminum wind chimes
- ❑ Nylon monofilament
- ❑ Needle-nose pliers
- ❑ #16 tapestry needle
- ❑ Hot-glue gun

Stitching Step by Step

1 Cut snowman head, two mittens, snowflake top and snowflake bottom from 7-count plastic canvas according to graphs.

2 Cut body front and back from plastic canvas radial circles according to graph, trimming away gray areas.

3 Stitch snowman head and mittens according to graphs, filling in uncoded area on head with white Continental Stitches and reversing one mitten before stitching; leave unstitched areas at cuffs of mittens as shown. Overcast head and mittens according to graphs.

4 When background stitching is complete, Backstitch and Straight Stitch snowman's mouth and work French Knot eyes using 1 ply separated from a length of black yarn, and wrapping yarn once around needle for each French Knot.

5 Overcast snowflake top and bottom using craft cord. Center and hot-glue snowflake top to bottom; set aside.

6 Stitch plastic canvas ring for body *front only* according to graph, noting unstitched area at top; back will remain unstitched. Hold back against reverse side of front; using white yarn, Whipstitch inner and outer edges.

Assembly

Note: Refer to photo throughout.

1 Cut four 4-inch (10.2cm) lengths of nylon monofilament. Thread one through hole in each chime.

2 Thread monofilament ends through body from front to back where indicated by blue dots on graph. Tie ends together, adjusting lengths to position chimes as desired. Add a dot of hot glue on each dot to secure; trim ends.

3 Hot-glue head to unstitched area on body front, hot-glue unstitched areas of mittens to back of body as shown, with thumbs toward head. Hot-glue snowflake to lower right area of snowman body.

4 *Earmuffs:* Wrap silver tinsel stem around pencil to curl; slide off. Glue ends of curled stem to sides of head so stem forms an arc above head as shown. Hot-glue pompoms to edge of head at ends of stem.

5 *Hanger:* Thread monofilament through center top edge of head; knot ends to form a small hanging loop.

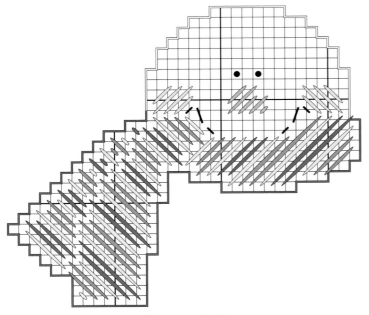

Snowman Head
33 holes x 29 holes
Cut 1

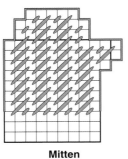

Mitten
11 holes x 13 holes
Cut 2, reverse 1

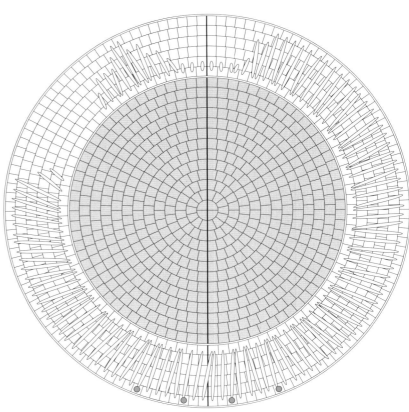

Snowman Body Front & Back
Cut 2, cutting away gray area
Stitch 1

Snowflake Top
9 holes x 9 holes
Cut 1

Snowflake Bottom
7 holes x 7 holes
Cut 1

Snowflake Trio

Designs by Ruby Thacker

Size: **Large Snowflake:** 4½ inches W x
5¾ inches H (11.4cm x 14.6cm)
Medium Snowflake: 3¾ inches W x
4½ inches H (9.5cm X 11.4cm)
Small Snowflake: 3¼ inches W x 4 inches H
(8.2cm x 10.2cm)

Skill Level: Beginner

Materials

❑ 3 Uniek QuickShape 5-inch plastic canvas hexagons
❑ Medium weight yarn with silver metallic wrap as
listed in color keys
❑ Crystal #006 acrylic faceted stones from
The Beadery:
    6 (10mm x 5mm) navettes
    12 (15mm x 7mm) navettes
    1 (13mm) round
    12 (7mm) rounds
❑ 3 small suction cups
❑ #16 tapestry needle
❑ Jewel glue

Stitching Step by Step

1 Cut plastic canvas hexagons according to graphs, cutting away gray areas, and leaving hexagon's original hanging loop intact for large snowflake. When cutting hexagons for small and medium snowflakes, include hanging loops according to graphs.

2 Stitch and Overcast snowflakes according to graphs.

3 Referring to graphs and photo, glue faceted stones to snowflakes as follows:

Large snowflake: Glue 6 (10mm x 5mm) navettes in center, and 6 (7mm) round stones to "points" of snowflake as shown.

Medium snowflake: Glue 6 (15mm x 7mm) navettes to "arms" of snowflake, and 13mm round stone in center as shown.

Small snowflake: Glue 6 (7mm) round stones to "points" of snowflake, and six (15mm x 7mm) navettes around center as shown.

4 Affix suction cups to window; suspend snowflakes from suction cups.

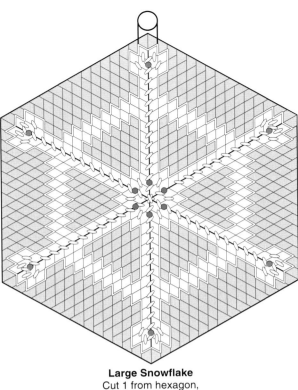

Large Snowflake
Cut 1 from hexagon,
cutting away gray areas

Hanger

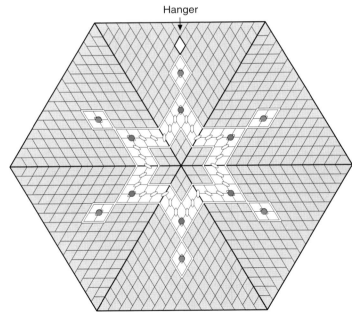

Small Snowflake
Cut 1 from hexagon,
cutting away gray areas

Hanger

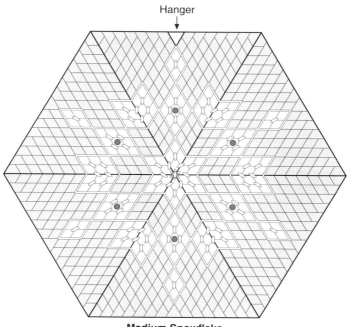

Medium Snowflake
Cut 1 from hexagon,
cutting away gray areas

COLOR KEY
MEDIUM SNOWFLAKE

Yards	**Medium Weight Yarn**
4 (3.7m)	☐ White with silver metallic wrap
	○ Attach 13mm round stone
	● Attach 15mm x 7mm navette

Sparkling Snowflakes

Designs by Angie Arickx

Size: **Suncatcher:** 5 inches W x 5 inches H
(12.7cm x 12.7cm)
Ornament: 5 inches W x 5 inches H x
5 inches D (12.7cm x 12.7cm x 12.7cm)
Skill Level: Beginner

Materials

❑ 4 Uniek QuickShape 5-inch plastic canvas hexagons
❑ Rainbow Gallery Plastic Canvas 7⅛-inch-wide
  metallic needlepoint yarn as listed in color key
❑ Suction cup with hook
❑ Nylon monofilament (optional)
❑ #16 tapestry needle

Stitching Step by Step

Suncatcher

1 Cut one snowflake from plastic canvas hexagon
according to graph, cutting away gray areas and
leaving the hexagon's original hanging loop intact.

2 Stitch plastic canvas according to graph, including
center stitches overlaying yellow line; Overcast
edges according to graph.

3 Affix suction cup to window; suspend snowflake
from suction cup.

Ornament

1 Cut one snowflake from plastic canvas hexagon
according to graph, cutting away gray areas and
leaving the hexagon's original hanging loop intact.

2 Cut two snowflakes from plastic canvas hexagons
according to graph, cutting away gray areas and
cutting off the hexagons' original hanging loop. Carefully
cut these snowflakes in half from top to bottom, cutting
along the groove in the center bar (yellow line on graph)
of plastic canvas.

3 Stitch all plastic canvas pieces according to
graph, leaving the straight center edges of the half
snowflakes unstitched, and omitting the center stitches
over the yellow line on the whole snowflake.

4 Whipstitch the straight edges of two half snowflakes
to each side of whole snowflake along its unstitched
center bar. Fan out edges of snowflake evenly.

5 Suspend snowflake from original hanging loop,
adding a loop of monofilament if desired.

Suncatcher
Cut 1 hexagon, cutting away gray areas

Ornament
Cut 3 hexagons, cutting away gray areas;
cut 2 snowflakes in half along
yellow line before stitching

COLOR KEY	
Yards	**Metallic Needlepoint Yarn**
38 (34.8m)	▨ White pearl #PC10
	╱ White pearl #PC10 Backstitch
Color number given is for Rainbow Gallery Plastic Canvas 7 metallic needlepoint yarn.	

Snowman Basket

Design by Chris Westerberg

Size: 10¾ inches W x 12¾ inches H x 2⅛ inches D
(27.3cm x 32.4cm x 5.4cm)
Skill Level: Beginner

Materials

- ❑ 2 sheets clear 7-count plastic canvas
- ❑ Uniek Needloft plastic canvas yarn as listed in color key
- ❑ #16 tapestry needle

Stitching Step by Step

1 Cut snowman basket back, front, two sides and hat from plastic canvas according to graphs. Cut also one piece 48 holes x 13 holes for basket bottom; it will remain unstitched.

2 Stitch plastic canvas according to graphs, noting that silver stitches are worked as Cross Stitches.

3 Overcast snowman back along side and top edges *outside arrows* using adjacent colors according to graph; Overcast hat using adjacent colors.

4 Using white yarn through step 5, Overcast top edges of basket front and sides.

5 Whipstitch bottom edges of basket back, front and sides to matching edges of unstitched basket bottom with right sides of basket back and front facing forward, and right sides of basket sides facing out.

6 Whipstitch adjacent edges of basket back, sides and front together along corners (between arrows), easing sides around curves.

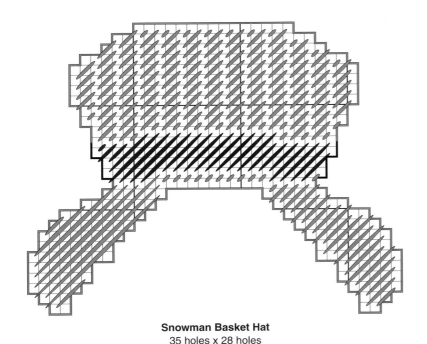

Snowman Basket Hat
35 holes x 28 holes
Cut 1

COLOR KEY	
Yards	**Plastic Canvas Yarn**
8 (7.4m)	■ Black #00
11 (10.1m)	■ Red #01
7 (6.5m)	■ Holly #27
12 (11m)	■ Royal #32
1 (1m)	■ Silver #37
60 (54.9m)	☐ White #41
8 (7.4m)	☐ Yellow #57
Color numbers given are for Uniek Needloft plastic canvas yarn.	

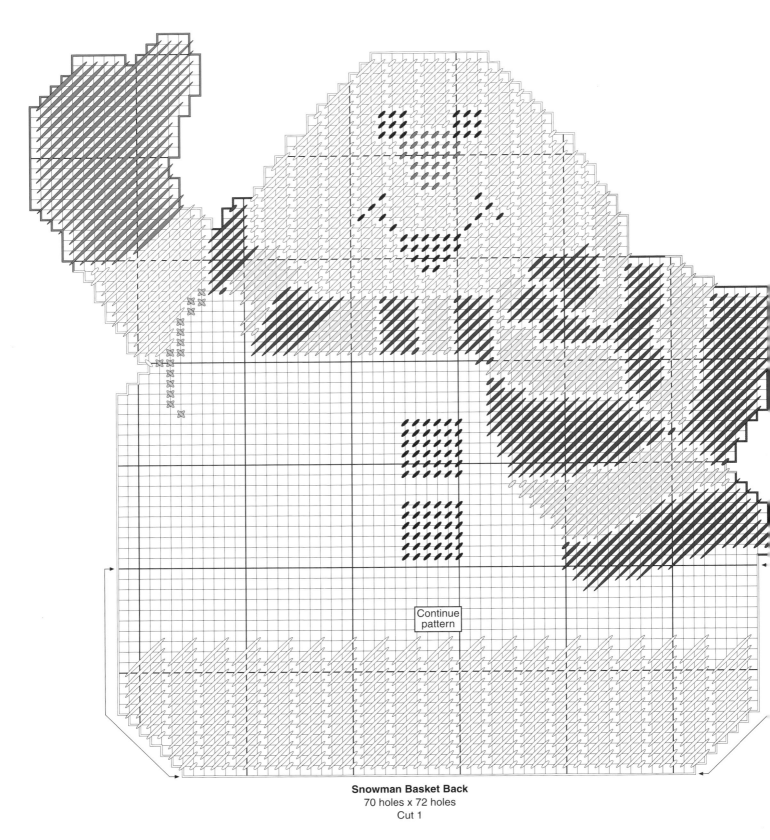

Snowman Basket Back
70 holes x 72 holes
Cut 1

Continue pattern

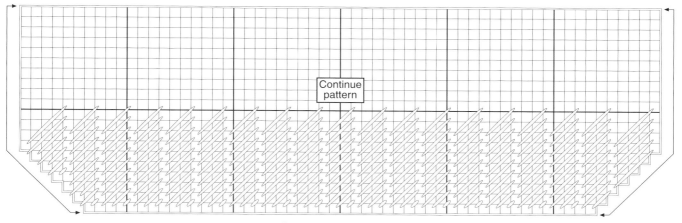

Snowman Basket Front
60 holes x 20 holes
Cut 1

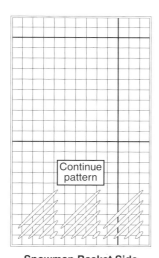

Snowman Basket Side
13 holes x 22 holes
Cut 2

COLOR KEY	
Yards	**Plastic Canvas Yarn**
8 (7.4m)	■ Black #00
11 (10.1m)	■ Red #01
7 (6.5m)	■ Holly #27
12 (11m)	■ Royal #32
1 (1m)	■ Silver #37
60 (54.9m)	□ White #41
8 (7.4m)	□ Yellow #57

Color numbers given are for Uniek
Needloft plastic canvas yarn.

Snow People

Designs by Angie Arickx

Size: **Tissue Topper:** Fits boutique-style tissue box
Napkin Holder: 7¼ inches W x 4 inches H x
2½ inches D (18.4cm x 10.2cm x 6.4cm)
Snowman Magnet: 2¼ inches W x
3⅛ inches H (5.7cm x 7.9cm)
Snow Woman Magnet: 2¼ inches W x
3 inches H (5.7cm x 7.6cm)
Snow Child Magnet: 1⅞ inches W x
2¼ inches H (4.8cm x 5.7cm)

Skill Level: Beginner

Materials

❏ 1½ sheets clear 7-count plastic canvas
❏ Uniek Needloft plastic canvas yarn as listed in
   color key
❏ 3 (1-inch/2.5cm) pieces magnet strip or
   3 button magnets
❏ #16 tapestry needle
❏ Hot-glue gun

Stitching Step by Step

Birdhouse Tissue Topper

1 Cut two pieces for tissue topper front/back, two tissue topper sides, two roof sides, two roof trim pieces, four chimney sides, eight small shutters, four large shutters, four perches, four snowmen and four snow women from plastic canvas according to graphs.

2 Stitch plastic canvas according to graphs, filling in uncoded areas with white Continental Stitches.

Tissue Topper Assembly

1 Using camel yarn, Overcast three edges of each perch, leaving one short edge unstitched. Whipstitch unfinished edges of perches to tissue topper front and back where indicated by red lines on front/back graph.

2 Using royal yarn, Whipstitch front, back and sides together along corners; Overcast top and bottom edges of tissue topper.

3 Overcast shutters using burgundy yarn. Referring to photo throughout, hot-glue short shutters beside black "openings" on front and back, positioning 5-hole edges of shutters next to openings. Hot-glue long shutters beside windows on sides.

Roof & Chimney

1 Using white yarn throughout, Overcast bottom edges of roof pieces. Overcast *vertical edges inside arrows only* of cutouts in top edge.

2 Align roof pieces with cutouts facing. Using dark royal yarn, Whipstitch roof pieces together along adjacent straight edges at top.

3 Using white yarn through step 4, Overcast bottom edge of roof trim pieces between dots. Whipstitch remaining edges of roof trim to ends of joined roof pieces.

4 Slide chimney into opening in roof as shown; Whipstitch opposite bottom edges of chimney to adjacent unfinished edges in roof cutout.

Finishing

1 Overcast snow people according to graphs. Backstitch mouths and work French Knot eyes using black yarn, wrapping yarn once around needle for French Knots.

2 Referring to photo throughout, hot-glue a snowman and snow woman to each side of tissue topper with bottom edges even.

3 Position roof on top of tissue topper; secure with hot-glue.

4 Place tissue box inside tissue topper; feed tissues through chimney.

Napkin Holder

1 Cut two napkin holder long sides, two short sides, two snowmen, two snow women and four snow children from plastic canvas according to graphs. Cut also one piece 44 holes x 14 holes for napkin holder bottom; it will remain unstitched.

2 Stitch plastic canvas according to graphs, filling in uncoded areas with white Continental Stitches, and Overcasting top edges of long and short sides with white yarn as you stitch.

3 Using royal yarn, Whipstitch long and short sides together at corners. Whipstitch assembled sides to bottom.

4 Overcast snow people according to graphs. Backstitch mouths and work French Knot eyes using black yarn, wrapping yarn once around needle for each knot.

5 Referring to photo throughout, hot-glue a snowman, snow woman and snow child to each long side of napkin holder with bottom edges even. Hot-glue a snow child to each short side of napkin holder.

Magnets

1 Cut snowman, snow woman and snow child from plastic canvas according to graphs.

2 Stitch snow people according to graphs, filling in uncoded areas with white Continental Stitches. Overcast edges according to graphs.

3 Backstitch mouths and work French Knot eyes using black yarn, wrapping yarn once around needle for each knot.

4 Hot-glue a magnet strip to the reverse side of each snow person.

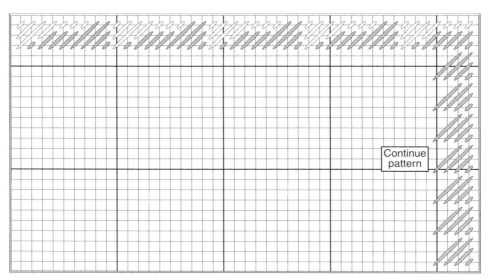

Continue pattern

Napkin Holder Long Side
44 holes x 25 holes
Cut 2

COLOR KEY	
Yards	**Plastic Canvas Yarn**
22 (20.1m)	■ Black #00
6 (5.5m)	■ Burgundy #03
9 (8.2m)	☐ Fern #23
108 (98.8m)	☐ Royal #32
73 (66.8m)	☐ White #41
2 (1.9m)	☐ Camel #43
15 (13.7m)	■ Dark royal #48
7 (6.5m)	☐ Watermelon #55
2 (1.9m)	☐ Bright orange #58
3 (2.8m)	☐ Bright blue #60
	Uncoded areas are white #41 Continental Stitches
✐	Black #00 Backstitch
●	Black #00 (1-wrap) French Knot
Color numbers given are for Uniek Needloft plastic canvas yarn.	

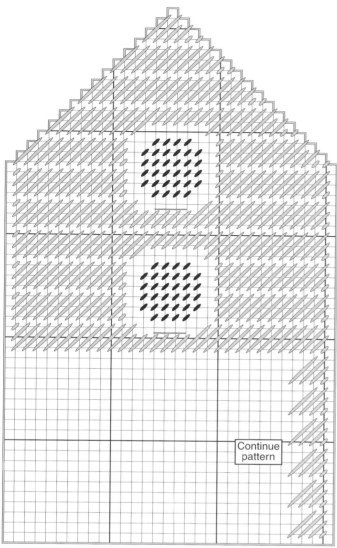

Birdhouse Tissue Topper Front/Back
31 holes x 52 holes
Cut 2

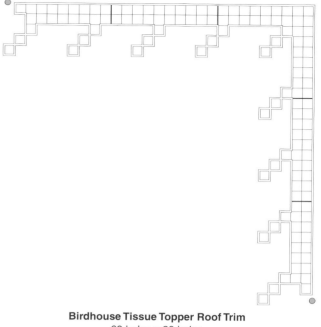

Birdhouse Tissue Topper Roof Trim
29 holes x 29 holes
Cut 2

Napkin Holder Short Side
14 holes x 25 holes
Cut 2

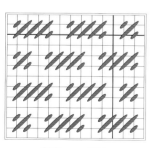

Chimney Side
13 holes x 12 holes
Cut 4 for
tissue topper

Perch
3 holes x 4 holes
Cut 4 for
tissue topper

Large Shutter
4 holes x 10 holes
Cut 4
for tissue topper

Small Shutter
3 holes x 7 holes
Cut 8 for
tissue topper

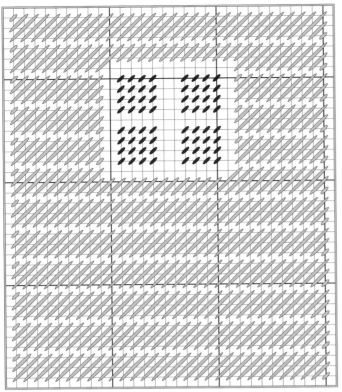

Birdhouse Tissue Topper Side
31 holes x 37 holes
Cut 2

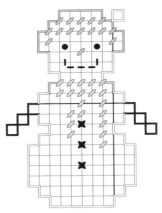

Snow Woman
14 holes x 19 holes
Cut 4 for tissue topper
Cut 2 for napkin holder
Cut 1 for magnet

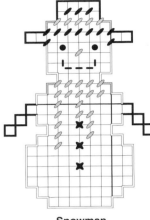

Snowman
14 holes x 20 holes
Cut 4 for tissue topper
Cut 2 for napkin holder
Cut 1 for magnet

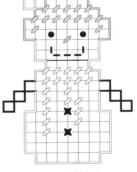

Snow Child
12 holes x 16 holes
Cut 4 for napkin holder
Cut 1 for magnet

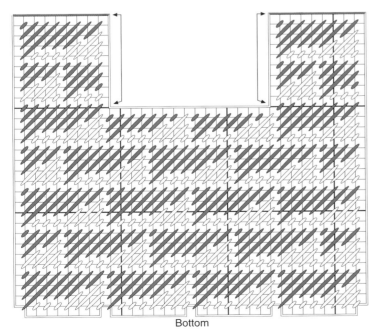

Birdhouse Tissue Topper Roof Side
33 holes x 29 holes
Cut 2

Bottom

COLOR KEY

Yards	Plastic Canvas Yarn
22 (20.1m)	■ Black #00
6 (5.5m)	■ Burgundy #03
9 (8.2m)	□ Fern #23
108 (98.8m)	□ Royal #32
73 (66.8m)	□ White #41
2 (1.9m)	□ Camel #43
15 (13.7m)	■ Dark royal #48
7 (6.5m)	■ Watermelon #55
2 (1.9m)	■ Bright orange #58
3 (2.8m)	□ Bright blue #60

Uncoded areas are white
#41 Continental Stitches

/ Black #00 Backstitch

● Black #00 (1-wrap) French Knot

Color numbers given are for Uniek Needloft plastic canvas yarn.

Candy Cane Train
& Ornaments

Designs by Carol Nartowicz

Size:
Train: 24½ inches W x 4¼ inches H x
3 inches D (62.2cm x 10.8cm x 7.6cm)
Candy Cane Ornament: 3¼ inches W x
5 inches H (8.3cm x 12.7cm)
Hard Candies Ornament: 3 inches W x
2½ inches H (7.6cm x 6.7cm), excluding
plastic wrap
Skill Level: Beginner

Candy Cane Train

Materials
- ❑ 7-count plastic canvas:
  - 3 sheets clear
  - ½ sheet white
- ❑ Uniek Needloft plastic canvas yarn as listed in color key
- ❑ 3 (4-inch/10.6cm) pieces Uniek Needloft white/silver #55008 craft cord
- ❑ #16 tapestry needle
- ❑ Hot-glue gun or craft glue

Stitching Step by Step
Cutting Plastic Canvas
1 From clear plastic canvas, cut two engine sides, engine nose, engine back, two engine roofs, engine cab front, two sleigh car sides, two snowman car sides, two snowman hats, two tree car sides, six car ends and 32 wheels according to graphs. Also cut one piece 30 holes x 16 holes for engine bottom and three pieces 34 holes x 16 holes for car bottoms; engine and car bottoms will remain unstitched.

2 From white plastic canvas, cut 12 candy cane backs according to graph; they will remain unstitched.

Engine
1 Stitch engine sides according to graph, reversing one engine side before stitching as a mirror image and filling in uncoded areas with yellow Continental Stitches. Overcast top of sides according to graphs.

2 Stitch engine nose, cab back, cab front and roofs according to graphs.

3 Using black, Whipstitch roof pieces together along two long edges; Overcast remaining long edges.

4 Referring to Engine Assembly diagram throughout, Whipstitch engine sides and engine cab back to each other along corners and to unstitched engine bottom. Whipstitch matching edges of engine nose and engine cab front together where indicated by blue arrows on graphs. Whipstitch joined cab front and nose to engine sides, easing engine nose around curved edges; Whipstitch edge of engine nose indicated by black arrows to front edge of unstitched bottom.

5 Thread the ends of one 4-inch (10.2cm) piece of craft cord through the engine cab back where indicated by blue dots on graph, leaving ends hanging evenly outside engine.

6 Position roof over top of engine cab as shown. Whipstitch front and back edges of roof to engine cab back and front using black yarn.

7 Stitch four wheels according to graph. Holding an unstitched wheel against the reverse side of a stitched wheel, Whipstitch edges together using royal. Repeat to Whipstitch unstitched wheels to remaining stitched ones. Hot-glue wheels to engine as shown, keeping bottom edges even.

Sleigh Car

1 Stitch sleigh car sides and two car ends according to graphs, using holly on ends and filling in uncoded areas on car sides with holly Continental Stitches.

2 Straight Stitch detail on sleighs using white yarn.

3 Using white yarn through step 4, Whipstitch an unstitched candy cane back to the reverse side of the matching top portion of each candy cane on car sides.

4 Without cutting white yarn and referring to photo throughout, Whipstitch car ends to car sides with bottom edges even.

5 Using holly yarn, Whipstitch joined car sides and ends to car bottom; Overcast unfinished top edges of car sides and ends.

6 Referring to step 7 for Engine, stitch and assemble four wheels; hot-glue wheels to car.

Snowman Car

1 Stitch snowman car sides, two car ends and snowman hats according to graphs, using dark royal on ends and filling in uncoded areas on car sides with dark royal Continental Stitches.

2 Using black yarn throughout, Straight Stitch snowmen mouths and hatbands on hats; work French Knot eyes, wrapping yarn once around needle.

3 Repeat steps 3 and 4 of Sleigh Car.

4 Using white yarn, Whipstitch joined car sides and ends to car bottom; using dark royal yarn, Overcast unfinished top edges of car sides and ends.

5 Referring to step 7 for Engine, stitch and assemble four wheels; hot-glue wheels to car. Hot-glue hats to snowmen as shown.

Tree Car

1 Stitch tree car sides and two car ends according to graphs, using yellow for ends and filling in uncoded areas on car sides with yellow Continental Stitches.

2 Using Christmas red, Straight Stitch decorations on trees.

3 Repeat steps 3 and 4 as for Sleigh Car.

4 Using yellow yarn, Whipstitch joined car sides and ends to car bottom; Overcast unfinished top edges of car sides and ends.

5 Referring to step 7 for Engine, stitch and assemble four wheels; hot-glue wheels to car.

Finishing

Join engine to desired car by threading ends of craft cord from engine (Engine, step 5) through car end where indicated by blue dots on car end graph; knot cord ends inside car. In the same manner, join remaining cars with craft cord.

Stitching Step by Step

Candy Canes

1 Cut 10 candy canes, five holly leaves and 15 holly berries from plastic canvas according to graphs.

2 Stitch five candy canes according to graphs; work Straight Stitches on candy canes using Christmas red yarn. Remaining candy canes will remain unstitched.

3 Holding one unstitched candy cane against the reverse side of a stitched candy cane, Whipstitch edges together using white yarn. Repeat to Whipstitch remaining unstitched candy canes to stitched ones.

4 Stitch holly leaves and berries according to graphs, Overcasting edges with matching colors as you stitch.

5 Referring to photo throughout, hot-glue a holly leaf and three berries to each candy cane.

Ornaments

Materials

Note: Materials and yarn amounts listed are sufficient to make a set of five candy canes and four hard candy ornaments.

❏ 1½ sheets clear 7-count plastic canvas
❏ Uniek Needloft plastic canvas yarn as listed in color key
❏ 1⅔ yards (1.5m) ⅜-inch-wide (10mm) red satin ribbon (optional)
❏ 9 wire ornament hooks (optional)
❏ Sewing needle and thread
❏ Clear plastic food wrap
❏ Hot-glue gun or craft glue

Hard Candies

1 Cut 36 hard candies and eight candy bases from plastic canvas according to graphs.

2 Stitch six hard candies according to graph. Stitch six more substituting Christmas red for royal, and four each substituting Christmas green, yellow and watermelon for royal yarn. Remaining hard candies will remain unstitched.

3 Holding one unstitched candy between the reverse sides of two matching stitched candies, Whipstitch edges together using matching yarn. Repeat to Whipstitch remaining unstitched candies between stitched ones.

4 Stitch four candy bases according to graph; remaining candy bases will remain unstitched.

5 Holding one unstitched candy base against the reverse side of a stitched candy base, Whipstitch edges together using white yarn. Repeat to Whipstitch unstitched candy bases to remaining stitched bases.

6 Cut 12 (5-inch/12.7cm) squares of plastic food wrap. Wrap a plastic square around each hard candy, twisting ends of plastic in opposite directions to secure.

7 Referring to photo throughout, cluster three wrapped hard candies atop each base; hot-glue in place.

Finishing

For garland, tie, stitch or glue hanging loop in each end of ribbon. Lay ribbon flat; arrange candy cane and hard candies ornaments on ribbon, spacing them evenly and alternating ornaments. Hot-glue or stitch ornaments to ribbon; suspend garland from loops.

For ornaments, thread a wire ornament hook through the top edge of each candy cane and of each hard candies base.

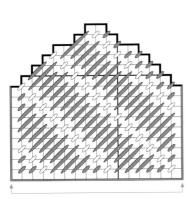

Engine Cab Front
16 holes x 15 holes
Cut 1

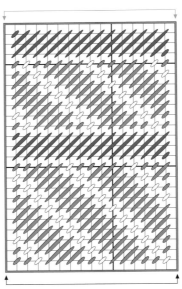

Engine Nose
16 holes x 24 holes
Cut 1 from clear

Engine Cab Back
16 holes x 27 holes
Cut 1 from clear

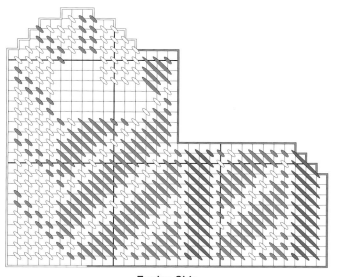

Engine Side
30 holes x 25 holes
Cut 2 from clear
Reverse 1 and stitch as mirror image

COLOR KEY
TRAIN

Yards	Plastic Canvas Yarn
5 (4.6m)	■ Black #00
34 (31.1m)	■ Christmas red #02
17 (15.6m)	■ Holly #27
5 (4.6m)	■ Royal #32
29 (26.6m)	□ White #41
	Uncoded areas on sleigh car are holly #27 Continental Stitches
15 (13.8m)	Uncoded areas on snowman car are dark royal #48 Continental Stitches
21 (19.3m)	Uncoded areas on engine and tree car are yellow #57 Continental Stitches
	╱ Dark royal #48 Overcast
	╱ Yellow #57 Overcast
	╱ Black #00 Straight Stitch
	╱ Christmas red #02 Straight Stitch
	╱ White #41 Straight Stitch
	● Black #00 (1-wrap) French Knot
	● Attach white/silver craft cord "coupler"

Color numbers given are for Uniek Needloft plastic canvas yarn.

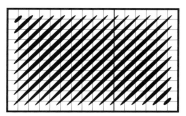

Engine Roof
16 holes x 10 holes
Cut 2 from clear

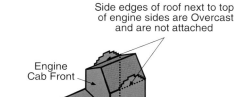

Side edges of roof next to top of engine sides are Overcast and are not attached

Engine Cab Front

Engine Nose

Engine Side

Engine Assembly

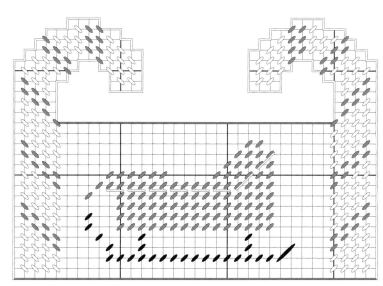

Sleigh Car
34 holes x 25 holes
Cut 2 from clear

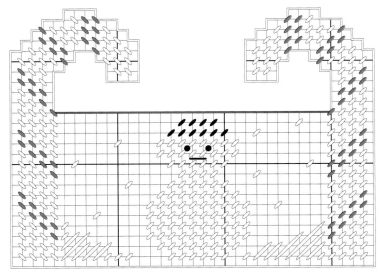

Snowman Car
34 holes x 25 holes
Cut 2 from clear

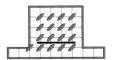

Snowman Hat
9 holes x 5 holes
Cut 2 from clear

Wheel
6 holes x 6 holes
Cut 32 from clear
Stitch 16

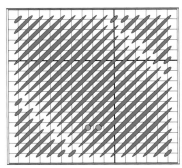

Car End
16 holes x 15 holes
Cut 6 from clear
Stitch 2 as shown for sleigh car
Stitch 2 each substituting dark royal for holly on
snowman car, and yellow for holly on tree car

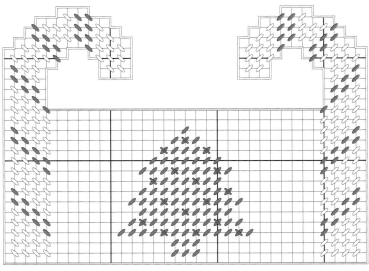

Tree Car
34 holes x 25 holes
Cut 2 from clear

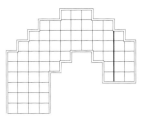

Train Candy Cane Back
12 holes x 10 holes
Cut 12 from white
Do not stitch

COLOR KEY	
TRAIN	
Yards	**Plastic Canvas Yarn**
5 (4.6m)	■ Black #00
34 (31.1m)	■ Christmas red #02
17 (15.6m)	■ Holly #27
5 (4.6m)	■ Royal #32
29 (26.6m)	□ White #41
	Uncoded areas on sleigh car are holly #27 Continental Stitches
15 (13.8m)	Uncoded areas on snowman car are dark royal #48 Continental Stitches
21 (19.3m)	Uncoded areas on engine and tree car are yellow #57 Continental Stitches
	⁄ Dark royal #48 Overcast
	⁄ Yellow #57 Overcast
	⁄ Black #00 Straight Stitch
	⁄ Christmas red #02 Straight Stitch
	⁄ White #41 Straight Stitch
	● Black #00 (1-wrap) French Knot
	● Attach white/silver craft cord "coupler"

Color numbers given are for Uniek Needloft plastic canvas yarn.

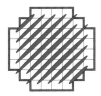

Hard Candy
8 holes x 8 holes
Cut 36
Stitch 6 as shown
Stitch 6 substituting
Christmas red for royal
Stitch 4 each substituting
Christmas green, yellow and
watermelon for royal;
12 remain unstitched

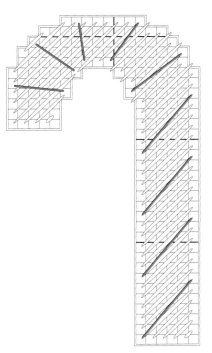

Candy Cane Ornament
18 holes x 32 holes
Cut 10; stitch 5

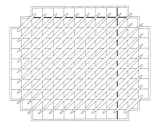

Hard Candies Base
13 holes x 11 holes
Cut 8; stitch 4

Holly Leaves
15 holes x 15 holes
Cut 5

COLOR KEY
ORNAMENTS

Yards	Plastic Canvas Yarn
13 (11.9m)	■ Christmas red #02
8 (7.4m)	■ Holly #27
5 (4.6m)	Christmas green #28
7 (6.4m)	■ Royal #32
29 (26.6m)	☐ White #41
5 (4.6m)	Watermelon #55
5 (4.6m)	☐ Yellow #57
	╱ Christmas red #02 Straight Stitch

Color numbers given are for Uniek
Needloft plastic canvas yarn.

Holly Berry
3 holes x 3 holes
Cut 15

The full line of The Needlecraft Shop
products is carried by Annie's Attic catalog.
TOLL-FREE ORDER LINE
or to request a free catalog
(800) 582-6643
Customer Service
(800) 449-0440
Visit AnniesAttic.com

We have made every effort to ensure the accuracy
and completeness of these instructions. We cannot,
however, be responsible for human error, typographical
mistakes or variations in individual work.

ISBN: 978-1-57367-312-9

Printed in USA

2 3 4 5 6 7 8 9

Shopping for Supplies

For supplies, first shop your local craft
and needlework stores. Some supplies
may be found in fabric, hardware and
discount stores. If you are unable to find
the supplies you need, please call Annie's
Attic at (800) 582-6643 to request a free
catalog that sells plastic canvas supplies.

Before You Cut

Buy one brand of canvas for each entire project as brands can di
fer slightly in the distance between bars. Count holes carefully from th
graph before you cut, using the bolder lines that show each 10 hole
These 10-count lines begin in the lower left corner of each graph t
make counting easier. Mark canvas before cutting; then remove all mark
completely before stitching. If the piece is cut in a rectangular or squar
shape and is either not worked, or worked with only one color an
one type of stitch, the graph is not included in the pattern. Instead, th
cutting and stitching instructions are given in the general instructions c
with the individual project instructions.

Covering the Canvas

Bring needle up from back of work, leaving a short length of yarn o
back of canvas; work over short length to secure. To end a thread, weav
needle and thread through the wrong side of your last few stitches; cli
Follow the numbers on the small graphs beside each stitch illustration; brin
your needle up from the back of the work on odd numbers and down throug
the front of the work on even numbers. Work embroidery stitches last, aft
the canvas has been completely covered by the needlepoint stitches.

Basic Stitches

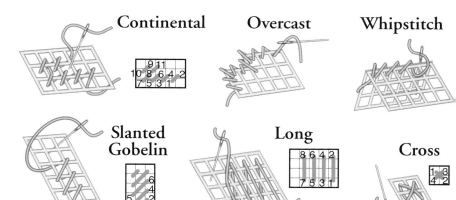

Continental
Overcast
Whipstitch
Slanted Gobelin
Long
Cross

Embroidery Stitches

French Knot
Lazy Daisy
Backstitch
Straight

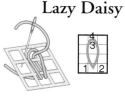

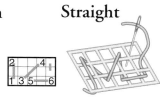

METRIC KEY:
millimeters = (mm)
centimeters = (cm)
meters = (m)
grams = (g)